Mouse Time!

A Disney Vacation Game and Activity Book

Chris Sylvester

Hunting Creek Press

ISBN-10: 0-9839282-3-1

ISBN-13: 978-0-9839282-3-2

IMPORTANT NOTICE

PARENTS/CHAPERONES: Always supervise children participating in the games and activities in this book.

CHILDREN: Always ask permission of your parents or chaperones before undertaking any of the games and activities in this book. Do not approach strangers without adult supervision.

DISCLAIMER

ACKNOWLEDGEMENTS

Thanks to Elizabeth Kelley for a great variety of valuable help. Thanks to my family, friends, and other Disney fans for offering their own unique tips and advice. Thanks to the Imagineers, Cast Members, and all people associated with the Walt Disney Company for creating these wonderful destinations and for always making a visit there so enjoyable.

To the entire Sylvester family for making each trip to Walt Disney World unforgettable.

Table of Contents

INTRODUCTION

Disney vacations are family trips for a lifetime with amazing attractions, comfortable accommodations, and fine dining. However, even during the most entertaining family vacations, there are unavoidable periods of boredom and waiting. This book is designed to enhance your visit to Walt Disney World by helping to overcome the inevitable waiting times and by adding fun to your overall experience.

Try some of these games and activities when you are waiting in line at an attraction, walking around the theme parks, or riding in a car, bus, or monorail to get to a park.

Theme Park and Attraction Specific Activities are in the beginning of the book for easy reference. Use an official Disney theme park map at each park to coordinate your visit with these specific games and activities. These games and activities can be completed at each park by following the general touring path formats described below. However, make sure to adjust and customize your touring plans to fit your goals, especially concerning the most popular attractions. The walking directions in this section follow the perspectives of the official maps.

MAGIC KINGDOM: To complete the activities, start in Main Street, U.S.A., then turn left to Adventureland and follow a circular path to the right through Frontierland to Liberty Square. Continue to the upper right to Fantasyland, New Fantasyland and finish in Tomorrowland.

EPCOT: To complete the activities follow a circular path to the right starting at Spaceship Earth and Innoventions in Future World. There are activities to the left at Mission Space and Test Track. To complete the activities at the World Showcase, start with the Mexico Pavilion and proceed in a semicircle to the right all the way to the Canada Pavilion. The final activities are below the Canada Pavilion to the left at the Land Pavilion and at the Seas with Nemo and Friends.

HOLLYWOOD STUDIOS: The activities begin as you walk down Hollywood Boulevard and take a left toward Echo Lake. The activities continue to the left at the Indiana Jones Stunt Spectacular and Star Tours. There are a variety of activities to the right in the Streets of America area. There are more activities heading to the right toward the Sorcerer's Hat, at Pixar Place, and continuing to the right at the Animation Courtyard.

The remaining activities are for the thrill attractions at the end of Sunset Boulevard at the bottom right of the theme park.

ANIMAL KINGDOM: To complete the activities, begin at Discovery Island and the Tree of Life, and then move straight up to Africa and to Rafiki's Planet Watch.

There are activities to the right in Asia continuing down to the right and finishing in DinoLand U.S.A.

The **General Waiting in Line Activities** will work well while waiting in any line. The **General Games and Activities** can be completed during your visit to any of the theme parks.

The **Anywhere Activities** will work well wherever you are. Try them when you are in transit, at the airport, in the hotel room, or waiting for your food to arrive at a restaurant.

Autograph Pages are included for use in the theme parks to both record signatures from Disney characters as well as to send messages to characters from fellow visitors. There are also **Disney Memories** pages at the back of the book for multiple children to complete at the end of each day or at the end of your visit.

Capturing this memorable information will serve as a treasured keepsake and a happy reminder of the highlights of your family's Disney vacation.

In addition, there is a section of **Helpful Disney Tips** at the end of the book that contains useful information about:

-Planning and timing your visit

-Theme park-specific tips and interactive programs

-Fun activities outside the theme parks

-Special holiday and seasonal events

While this book is designed primarily for use by visitors to Walt Disney World and its four theme parks, the general and anywhere activities and games will also work well at other Disney parks, Disney cruises, and Disney attractions around the world.

GAMES & ACTIVITIES

The games and activities in this book vary in difficulty and in the time and effort required to complete them. Some can be done quickly as you are waiting for an attraction while others might require some effort during the entire day at the theme park.

If you are having trouble completing a task or finding the answer to a question, consult the **Answer Key for Selected Activities** near the end of the book starting on page 197. You can also always ask a nearby Disney Cast Member (any Disney employee is considered a Cast Member at Disney World) for assistance. Some of the activities will require the Answer Key or Cast Member input. Cast Members are unfailingly polite and helpful and will either provide you with the answer or find someone who can assist you.

To make some activities harder or easier, you can adjust the number of examples you must find or change the time limit.

As you will be at one of the world's most famous destinations celebrating creativity and imagination, try adding your own personal twists to some of these activities. Make an effort to create similar and new games of your own.

Remember that the main point of these activities is to have more fun interaction at Disney with your family or group.

Have a magically great time!

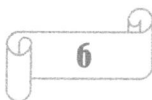

Theme Park and Attraction Specific Activities

MAGIC KINGDOM

<u>1</u>

Upon entering the **Magic Kingdom**:

a.   Take out an official park map and have everyone predict the area of the park where they will first encounter Mickey Mouse greeting people. You can also predict how long it will take until the group finds Mickey. The closest guesses win. Play this game with other Disney characters and at other parks, too!

b.   Go to the **Main Street Station** of the **Walt Disney World Railroad**. In the lower area, find the Train Bulletin Board with a list of arriving and departing trains. Why is the train from Grizzly Flats delayed?

c.   In the waiting area on the train track level, find a large antique music box and see

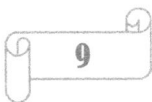

if you can make it play a song. In this area, listen for the sound of a telegraph machine typing a special message in Morse code.

d.   If you ride on a train, ask the conductor what the name of the locomotive is and how old it is. Find out what the locomotive's top speed in miles per hour (mph) is.

e.   Ask the conductor if you can be a guest conductor and make the "All aboard!" announcement.

2

In Main Street, U.S.A:

a.   Find a bench with a colorful statue of Goofy happily sitting on it. See what interesting thing happens when you sit down next to him.

b.   Work together or play a game to be the first to find the paw prints of Lady and the Tramp outside of **Tony's Town Square Restaurant**. Find a silhouette of the couple eating their romantic spaghetti and meatballs dinner at the back of the restaurant.

c.   In the Town Square, find the bench with bronze statues of Roy Disney, Walt's brother, and Minnie Mouse. Sit next to them for a photo.

d.   Find the antique phone in the **Chapeau** hat shop and listen to some interesting conversations.

e.   Work together to find the **Harmony Barber Shop**. Children who are receiving their first hair cut can get a complimentary certificate with a lock of hair and a special Mickey Ears hat.

At certain times a real barbershop quartet will be there to entertain you! The Harmony Barber Shop also has lots of pixie dust to share.

f.   Walk toward **Cinderella Castle** to the circular area known as the **Hub.** Find the famous statue of Walt Disney with Mickey Mouse called *Partners*.

Which figure in the statue has bigger ears and feet?

For those with good eyes and cameras with zooming ability: see if Walt is wearing rings on both hands. Does one of the rings resemble Mickey?

g.   How many small statues can you find around the *Partners* statue? How many Disney characters can you identify?

$\underline{\mathbf{3}}$

Write down the names of the different **Lands** you explore during your visit to the **Magic Kingdom**. Determine whether there is anywhere you can have one foot in one Land and one in another or if the Lands are in their own distinct and separate areas.

Do you notice any difference in the color of the pavement beneath your feet and any other changes when you enter different Lands?

4

If your group likes thrill rides, try to experience each of the following attractions during your visit to the Magic Kingdom: **Splash Mountain, Big Thunder Mountain Railroad,** and **Space Mountain.**

After completing each attraction, form a family circle and say, "We conquered _____!"

Celebrate with hugs and high fives!

<u>5</u>

In **Adventureland:**

a.   Find the only country's flag other than the United States flag flying at a Magic Kingdom attraction. At which attraction did you find it? Which country does it represent?

b.   At **Aladdin's Magic Carpet Ride,** find a golden camel spitting water on visitors. How many humps does the camel have?

c.   Find some sparkling jewels embedded in the concrete near Aladdin's Magic Carpet Ride.

6

At the **Jungle Cruise:**

a.   In line, find the unusual name of the employee of the month on a green sign.

b.   Find a tarantula in a cage and see if you can make it move.

c.   Find a ripped t-shirt advertising "free kittens." What type of kittens do you think they are?

d.   Find the crew mess lunch menu board with some interesting food items. Which one sounds the least appetizing?

e.   During the ride, write down or memorize your favorite and least favorite jokes that the guide tells.

f.   Upon exiting the ride, find a chalkboard with some unusual names of missing passengers and overdue boats from earlier cruises.

g.   Write down or memorize the name of your boat and guide. After the ride, make up funny names for a new boat with a new guide.

Boat Name

_____

Guide Name

_____

New Boat Name

_____

New Guide Name

_____

7

At the **Pirates of the Caribbean:**

a.   At the front of the attraction, find a parrot that looks like a pirate, complete with a pirate hat and an eye patch.

b.   Count the number of cannons and cannonballs you see in line and during the attraction.

c.   If you are on the right side of the line, find a spooky chess game being played by two pirate skeletons. Who is winning the game?

Just before you climb aboard the boat, listen for the sound of a pirate digging for treasure.

d.   Sing this familiar line from a pirate song a few times: "Yo ho, yo ho, a pirate's life for me!" Did anyone join in or encourage you?

e.   Complete this famous pirate phrase that you will hear on the ride: "Dead men tell

_____."

f.   Find the pirate footprints on the moving walkway as you exit. Why are they unusual?

8

In Frontierland at Splash Mountain:

a.   Predict who in your party will get the wettest during the ride and who will stay the driest. The closest guesses win.

b.   In the waiting area, find the bird and chipmunk houses and listen for some animated conversations among the little critters.

c.   How many Br'er animals are found at this attraction? Some signs will help you. Write their names down here:

_____

_____

_____

What word is Br'er an abbreviation for?

_____

9

At Big Thunder Mountain Railroad:

a.   Find a sign that shows how often miners can get meals and baths. Does this sound appealing to you?

b.   Try out the blasting machines. What was your favorite blasting location?

c.   Look through the subterrascope to see what is happening underground. Is anyone stealing gold from the mine?

d.   After the ride, find a crate labeled Lytum & Hyde Explosives Company.

e.   As you are exiting the attraction, find some bubbling geysers. Wait for the geysers to erupt with steam and water shooting out of the ground.

10

On the way to and at **Liberty Square:**

a.   Find the claw marks in the waiting area of the **Country Bear Jamboree** in Frontierland. Who do you think made these marks?

b.   Find the **Liberty Square Liberty Tree.** How many lanterns are hanging on it? What do they represent? Find the two lighted lanterns in the upstairs window of a nearby building? What historic event do they represent?

c.   Find the replica of the **Liberty Bell.** What unusual physical feature does it have? Where is the original located?

d.   While waiting for the **Hall of Presidents,** guess which presidents will have speaking roles. Find artifacts belonging to President Washington and at least two other presidents, as well as dresses worn by First Ladies.

e.   After the show, have the group vote on which presidents looked the most and least lifelike.

11

Outside and in line at the **Haunted Mansion**:

a.   Find signs of an invisible horse near the black hearse carriage.

b.   Go to the left to experience the amazing interactive queue. Try to solve the mystery of who killed whom when looking at the first five busts that you encounter. The clues are found in the brass plates attached to the stands supporting the busts. These plates contain inscriptions with clues, along with symbols of the killing instruments associated with the characters. Start with Uncle Jacob's bust in the middle and end with Cousin Maude's. Look for the cause of her demise found somewhere in her hair bun.

c.   Find the Composer's Crypt. Play the pipe organ, find a raven, and touch other instruments on the front and back of the crypt and see what happens. Find a one-eyed cat and see what happens when you touch it.

d.   Does Master Gracey's tombstone have a flower on top of it?

e.   Find the Sea Captain's Crypt and the Crypt of the Poetess. What unusual things happen at these crypts?

f.   Find the mansion bride's ring embedded in the pavement somewhere near the Sea Captain's Crypt.

g.   Push some books into the bookshelves in the Library Crypt. What happened? Find some symbols conveying a secret message on some of the books. If you are skilled at puzzles, take pictures of the symbols as a whole and try to crack the code later.

h.   Find the footprints and paw prints of the mansion's caretaker and his dog. Look near a gate with a lower door designed for dogs.

i.   Find the tombstone for Madame Leota. Does anything unusual happen when you look at Leota?

j.   When exiting the attraction, look to your left to find the pet cemetery on the hill. Find the small statue in the back of the pet cemetery honoring the Disney character Mr. Toad. Ask a Cast Member which current Disney attraction replaced Mr. Toad's Wild Ride.

12

While waiting in **Fantasyland** play a game to see who can answer the following questions the fastest:

a.   Who is the fairest one of them all? What magical object answers this question?

b.   What vegetable and animals magically became Cinderella's horse-drawn coach?

c.   How many dwarfs are there and what are their names? Which one doesn't have a beard?

d.   Where does Cinderella get her name?

e.   What type of poisoned fruit causes Snow White to fall into a deep sleep?

f.   After completing this game, work together to find **Willie the Giant** somewhere in **Sir Mickey's Gift Shop**.

13

While at "it's a small world:"

a.　Ask 5-10 people in line how many times they have been on the ride. Has anyone been on it more than ten times? Are any of the people from other countries?

b.　Sing or hum softly the chorus of the song "It's a Small World (After All)" for 30 seconds. Lyrics are on page 167. Did anyone in line join you?

c.　Find representations of the Eiffel Tower, the Leaning Tower of Pisa, and a windmill among the buildings in the queue area.

d.　During the attraction, make a checkmark or keep a count of how many different countries are represented by the singing children. What was your favorite exotic animal that you saw during the attraction?

e.　After the attraction, write down your favorite and least favorite costumes and your favorite and least favorite dances or celebrations.

14

At **Peter Pan's Flight**:

a. Find a scary creature holding a lantern above the FASTPASS sign. What is his name and what makes him different than other animals like him? Which character in the *Peter Pan* story fears him the most and why?

b. See if you can spot the scary creature above, Tinker Bell, and Ariel the Little Mermaid at different points during the ride.

c. According to the story, what magical thing makes it possible for the children (and your ship during the ride) to fly?

d. Where does Peter Pan live and what is the band of boys that live with him called?

e. Which city do you fly over at the beginning of the ride?

15

While at **Mickey's PhilharMagic**:

a.   Count the number of instruments painted on the walls. Are there more brass or string instruments?

b.   Find movie posters featuring Wheezy the Penguin, Genie, and Ariel. Which poster is your favorite?

c.   Which famous animated Disney film features Mickey Mouse as a sorcerer's apprentice performing magical acts? This film is famous for its skillful use of classical music to make the story vividly come to life.

d.   After the show, find the front half of Donald Duck somewhere in the gift shop.

16

At **Prince Charming's Regal Carrousel**:

a.   Have everyone in the group guess how many horses are on the carrousel. Ask a Cast Member how many horses there are or use the answer key to see who had the closest guess.

b.   Play a game to see who will be the first to find Cinderella's horse. It is rumored that her horse has a special golden ribbon on the tail.

c.   Write down another popular name for a carrousel/carousel:

_____

17

At the **Many Adventures of Winnie the Pooh:**

a.   Count the number of honey pots you can find before getting on the ride.

b.   Find a carved drawing of the *Nautilus* submarine over a doorway in Pooh's tree home. Why do you think it's there?

c.   See what happens when you knock on a storybook page in Pooh's residence that says "Please knock."

d.   Do some drumming on some musical pumpkins and spin some huge sun flowers.

e.   Figure out how to make some gophers pop out of their hiding places.

f.   Draw shapes with your hand against the Hunny Wall. Can you find objects or characters hidden behind this wall of dripping honey?

g.   In the beginning of the ride as you enter Owl's residence, see if you can spot a painting of a toad handing Owl a written document.

The painting is on the left hand side as you enter the residence. See the answer key for an explanation of this painting.

h. Find out how Pooh spells "honey" and write it below. Does he misspell some other words?

_____

i. What famous expression does Winnie the Pooh say when he is annoyed by something?

_____

18

At the **Mad Tea Party:**

a.   Have everyone guess which colors your group's Tea Cups will be.

b.   Play a game where everyone predicts who in the group will be the dizziest after the ride is over.

c.   Test who is the dizziest in the group after the ride. Have everyone try to walk in a straight line for ten steps and see who has the most trouble accomplishing this task. Make sure you only conduct this test in a relatively non-crowded area!

<u>19</u>

With the opening of **New Fantasyland,** count how many castles there are currently in the Magic Kingdom.

Write down the names of the Disney characters that have their own castles in the Magic Kingdom.

_____

_____

_____

20

While in **New Fantasyland,** see who can find the following items first or work together to find them:

a.   A fountain with one character standing on another. Who are they and what Disney animated movie are they from?

b.   Gargoyles. How many can you find during your visit? Do they all look the same?

c.   Chalk marks on the ceiling of the **Big Top Souvenirs** store. Which type of performers do you think put them up so high?

21

At **Maurice's Cottage** and **Enchanted Tales with Belle**:

a.   Find examples of Maurice's attempts at new inventions inside and outside. Which is your favorite?

b.   Find some marks on the wall showing Belle's height. How tall was she at your age? What is the French word for years?

c.   Find a book with a bite taken out of it. What type of animal do you think chewed on it?

d.   What object in the workshop becomes a magical portal for the group? Where does it take you?

e.   Think of an interesting question to ask Belle during the program. Which roles did you and your group members play?

22

While in line for **Under the Sea~Journey of the Little Mermaid:**

a.   Find an artistic representation of Ariel somewhere on the shipwreck near the entrance to the attraction.

b.   Count the number of waterfalls. Are there any sea creatures on the walls?

c.   Find a carving of the *Nautilus* submarine above one of the tidal pools.

d.   Find some treasure chests and ship steering wheels in the indoor queue area.

e.   Which type of human objects belonging to Scuttle the Seagull did you help the animated little crabs remove?

f.   What object is Scuttle holding in the queue area? Does this change at the beginning of the ride?

23

While waiting for **Dumbo the Flying Elephant** in the **Storybook Circus** Area:

a. In the Storybook Circus area, take a ride on the human cannonball slide.

b. Figure out how to light up the pretend fire in the burning building.

c. Play a game where everyone predicts the colors of the Dumbo cars they and everyone else will ride in.

d. Which type of bird is carrying the baby Dumbo at the top of the ride?

e. Find artificial peanuts in the pavement near the ride.

24

While in **Tomorrowland:**

a. Work together or play a game to be the first to find a moving, talking trash can named **PUSH**, who appears occasionally in the area. Think up some interesting questions to ask him and see how he responds.

Cast Members at City Hall or in Tomorrowland can inform you of the general times and locations where PUSH will be entertaining guests.

b. Find the futuristic phone booth with the **Metrophone** in Rockettower Plaza. Pick up the phone and listen to some interesting out of this world messages.

25

While waiting at **Buzz Lightyear's Space Ranger Spin:**

a.   Have everyone guess which player will finish with the highest score. After the ride, all players should congratulate one another for a good effort no matter what they score.

b.   Which intergalactic organization does Buzz Lightyear serve? What's the name of his unit? Complete his signature phrase "To infinity and _____!"

c.   Who is the evil leader that Buzz Lightyear has to defeat? What type of creatures will you have to fight to help Buzz?

d.   Where does Buzz want to rendezvous or meet after the mission is complete?

e.   If your group also played **Toy Story Midway Mania!** at **Hollywood Studios,** see if the same person scored the highest at both attractions.

26

In line at **Space Mountain:**

a.   What is the official Starport number for Space Mountain?

b.   Determine if there are more active lunar stations or Earth stations by viewing the Starport monitor system near the attraction entrance.

c.   Find some planets from our solar system on the sector charts located on the left hand side of the queue.

d.   What kind of threat do you protect the space ship from in the training session area? Who in your group did the best job protecting the space ship?

e.   On your way out of the attraction, find your group on a video display and see how everyone's faces look after this thrilling ride.

f.   Before you reach the exit, find a display area advertising a new luxury residential development far from the planet Earth.

What is the development's name and their catchy slogan?

_____

Will your butler be human or a robot? Would you like to live there or would you prefer to stay in your home on Earth?

EPCOT

27

Upon entering **EPCOT**:

a.   Find out what EPCOT stands for and write it here:

E _____

P _____

C _____

O _____

T _____

b.   Have each family member make up a combination of words using the first letters E, P, C, O, and T. Decide on the funniest example and write it here:

_____

28

While looking at **Spaceship Earth:**

a.   Have everyone in the group guess how tall in feet it is or how many stories it has. Also, have everyone guess how much it weighs. The closest guesses win.

b.   Which type of sports ball does it resemble?

c.   The group should give extra congratulations to anyone who can name what type of geometric shape Spaceship Earth is.

<u>29</u>

If your group likes thrill rides, try to experience each of the following attractions at EPCOT: **Test Track, Mission: SPACE,** and **Soarin'.**

After completing each attraction, form a family circle and say, "We conquered _____!"

Celebrate with hugs and high fives.

30

While visiting **Future World** and **Innoventions,**
find these unusual water fountains:

a.   Find the **Fountain of Nations** at
Innoventions Plaza and watch a musical
water ballet.

b.   Find the drinking fountain that
entertains you with sound effects while you
drink from it. It is located outside the Mouse
Gear Shop in Future World.

c.   Find the **Leaping Water Fountains** near
Journey into Imagination with Figment.
Predict where the water will leap to next.

*Because of the walking distance between
activities b and c, you can also save c until
after the completion of the upcoming World
Showcase activities.*

31

While visiting **Future World** and **Innoventions**, complete these activities:

a. Find a talking pink trash can in the **Electric Umbrella** restaurant in **Innoventions East**.

b. Try out the **Gesture Wall** and play the **Icons of Progress** touch screen game in the **IBM Think Exhibit** in **Innoventions West**. Try to win a free souvenir button by placing the icons in correct historical order.

c. Find **Club Cool** near Innoventions West and sample free Coca-Cola products from around the world. Which countries' beverages were your favorites and least favorites?

Only people with adventurous taste buds should try the Beverly from Italy!

32

At **Mission: SPACE,** complete these activities:

a.   Find out the name of the organization training you about space flight.

b.   Find a picture of the First Family in Space. Could your family get along on an extended space flight?

c.   Find out the name of your space vehicle and to which planet you will be traveling.

d.   Decide who will be the Navigator, Pilot, Commander, and Engineer on the flight. Did everyone complete their assigned duties during the mission? If you go on this attraction again, make sure everyone plays a different role.

e.   Outside Mission: SPACE, find the scale model of the Moon. What do the colored markings on it represent?

f.   What was the date that astronauts first landed on the Moon? Was anyone in your group alive when this historic event happened?

g.   If people in the group were old enough to remember the event, ask them to tell you about what it was like to watch the first men land on the Moon.

Were they and their family members and friends confident this historic but dangerous mission would be successful?

33

At **Test Track,** complete these activities:

a.   Find out the name of the car company that runs this extensive test track. Does anyone in your group own a car or truck made by this company?

b.   Work together to design an extra special car at the interactive terminals before the ride. See how your design is evaluated by the computer at the end of your ride. Where was your design strongest and where did it need the most improvement?

c.   Have everyone in the group guess the fastest speed your car will travel in miles per hour (mph) during the ride. Did anyone come within 5 mph of the correct answer?

d.   Have everyone in the group vote on their favorite real cars displayed in the showroom after the ride.

While visiting the **World Showcase,** match the following country pavilions with their specific attractions:

A. Norway _____

B. Mexico _____

C. China   _____

D. France _____

Gran Fiesta Tour

Reflections

Impressions

Maelstrom

Which country pavilion and attractions were your favorites?

35

While visiting the **World Showcase:**

a.   Count the number of countries and continents you visit. Pick up an **EPCOT Passport** or use your own notebook to track your travels with ink stamps and stickers from the different countries you visit.

b.   Open some crates in the **Outpost** area and see what happens. Try out some African drums. Find some scary masks and colorful beads.

c.   Learn how to say hello and thank you in at least two foreign languages. Try the phrases out with native speakers at the country pavilions.

d.   Attend an amazing performance of the **Jeweled Dragon Acrobats** at the China Pavilion.

e.   Find the miniature village and model train track at the Germany Pavilion.

f.   Find **Miyuki, a master of Japanese Candy Art,** near the Japan Pavilion. Ask her to make your favorite animal out of rice dough.

g.   Take in a unique audio-animatronic performance by the mouse named **Chef Remy** from *Ratatouille* at Les Chefs de France restaurant. Check on show times to make sure you see him in action.

h.   Find your way out of the **Hedge Maze** at the United Kingdom Pavilion.

i.   Count the totem poles at the Canada Pavilion.

j.   See how many group members you can comfortably fit in the red telephone booths at the Canada Pavilion.

36

Complete these activities at **Soarin'**:

a.   While waiting, guess which U.S. state you will be hang gliding over and see when you can first identify the state during the ride.

b.   Guess three fun activities or sports that people will be doing as you fly over them during the ride. The person with the most correct guesses wins.

c.   Write down your three favorite activities and things you saw during Soarin'.

d.   Make some creative suggestions for new places to fly over or activities to see in the next version of Soarin'.

37

At the **Seas with Nemo and Friends,** see who can find the following types of sea life first:

a. A manatee
b. A dolphin
c. Nemo and Dory (how many times?)
d. A sea urchin
e. A pufferfish
f. A sea horse
g. A hermit crab
h. An eel
i. A starfish
j. A jellyfish
k. A stingray
l. A shark
m. A sea turtle

Write down some other interesting sea animals you see:

_____

_____

_____

Which type of huge sea animal do you ride in during the attraction?

_____

Find a display featuring Bruce the Shark. See how many people you can fit comfortably in his huge jaws.

38

While at **Turtle Talk with Crush:**

a.   Find a happy starfish on the wall.

b.   Count the number of sharks and rays you see in the waiting area pools.

c.   Work together to decide on one question to ask Crush if you are called on during the show. Did Crush and the audience like it?

d.   What does Crush call our hands and our shirts? What does he call kids? What's the most popular word in the turtle language? What are his favorite expressions? Which one did you like the most?

_____

_____

_____

_____

e. What type of large ocean dweller makes life a little uncomfortable for Dory during the show?

_____

f. What were the most interesting things you learned about Crush and the other marine life in the show?

_____

_____

g. Make up a funny expression that Crush would use.

_____

HOLLYWOOD STUDIOS

<u>39</u>

Upon entering **Hollywood Studios:**

a.   Find three characters you recognize from movies or television walking around the park. The first person to find three wins.

b.   Make up an idea for a brief science fiction, romantic, or action adventure story involving your family that you think Walt Disney would like. Make sure you can explain your idea to someone in under a minute.

40

During your time at **Hollywood Studios,** if your group likes thrill rides, try to experience each of the following attractions: **Rock 'n Roller Coaster with Aerosmith, Twilight Zone Tower of Terror,** and **Star Tours-The Adventures Continue.**

After each attraction, form a family circle and say, "We conquered _____!"

Celebrate with hugs and high fives.

41

Find **Min and Bill's Dockside Diner** located in a ship in **Echo Lake**.

Work together to find and write down some famous names and addresses from classic movies written on the nearby crates.

The older folks and classic film fans in the group will be the most valuable players for this exercise.

42

Before entering the **Indiana Jones Epic Stunt Spectacular show,** find a well with a sign saying "Warning! Do ~~not~~ pull rope." Locate some nearby crates in the bushes marked "Don't Open."

What happened when you pulled on the rope and tried to open the crates?

43

At **Star Tours-The Adventures Continue:**

a.   Find an Imperial Walker and a Speeder Bike outside the attraction. Sit stylishly on the Speeder Bike.

b.   Count how many times you see the droids C-3PO and R2-D2 in person and on video while waiting for the ride to begin.

c.   What are some of the interesting items the scanning droid finds in the checked luggage?

d.   Try to spot a Wookie in the pre-flight safety video. Did you see any other interesting passengers in the video?

44

Complete the following activities during your visit to **Hollywood Studios**:

a.   Find a key under the welcome mat at the entrance of the **Muppet Vision 3D** show. A sign will tell you that it's there.

b.   Find out what unpleasant thing happens when you put your hand under the huge dog nose at the **Honey, I Shrunk the Kids Movie Set Adventure**.

c.   Find an umbrella attached to a streetlight in the **Streets of America** area, walking back toward and to the left of the **Lights, Motors, Action! Extreme Stunt Show**. This prop was inspired by the classic movie *Singin' in the Rain*. What do you think will happen when you pull on the handle of the umbrella? Try it and see if you were right.

d.   Find the handprints, footprints, and signatures of famous stars in front of the **Chinese Theater**. How many do you and the older people in the group recognize? Are any Disney, Star Wars, or Muppet characters represented? This area serves as the entrance to the **Great Movie Ride**.

e.   In the queue to the **Great Movie Ride**, find real props and items from famous movies. Which one was your favorite?

45

While waiting for **Toy Story Midway Mania!**:

a.   Have everyone guess which player will get the highest score during the ride.

b.   In line, identify at least three oversized objects representing classic children's games.

c.   Which colors are the hanging monkeys? Which children's game do they come from?

d.   Which Toy Story character is the Boardwalk Barker? What was his funniest remark? Which body part does he take off and put back on his face?

e.   After the ride, all players should congratulate one another for a good effort no matter what they score.

f.   If your group also played **Buzz Lightyear's Space Ranger Spin** at the Magic Kingdom, see if the same person scored the highest at both attractions.

46

At the **Magic of Disney Animation:**

a.   Attend the **Animation Academy** and see if you can learn to draw your favorite Disney character. Could anyone in your group succeed as a famed Disney animator?

b.   Play the interactive game with Lumière to find out which Disney character you are most like. Have everyone in the family guess their answer for themselves and other family members before they play. Were the results similar to the guesses?

47

At the Rock 'N Roller Coaster Starring Aerosmith:

a.   Find an upside down car somewhere outside near the entrance.

b.   Count how many strings the huge guitar in front of the ride has. What type of guitar is it?

c.   Have everyone in the group select one Aerosmith song they think they will hear during the ride. Older fans can help younger ones choose a popular song. At the end of the ride, see whose chosen songs were played.

d.   Count how many guitars, drums, keyboards, and other instruments are displayed in the recording studio during the pre-show.

e.   Which type of guitar does the guitarist Joe Perry ask the assistant to bring as the group is leaving the studio?

f.   What type of luxury vehicle are you riding in during the attraction?

48

At the **Twilight Zone Tower of Terror:**

a. See who can make the closest guesses to how many stories the building has and how many stories you will fall during the ride.

b. Have everyone try to imitate the eerie theme music sounds from *The Twilight Zone* television show.

c. Find out what scary event happened that made this hotel into a supernatural location. What night and year did it happen?

d. What type of bird sculpture serves as the centerpiece of the hotel lobby?

e. Have fans of *The Twilight Zone* television show do their best impressions of the distinctive voice and mannerisms of Rod Serling, the creator and host of the show. A skilled Rod Serling impersonator will appear on the monitors to provide players with inspiration.

f.   Ask fans of the show to discuss the plots of some of their favorite classic episodes. Many of these episodes have surprise endings.

If you plan on watching some of these episodes when you return home, don't let anyone tell you what happens at the end!

ANIMAL KINGDOM

49

Upon entering **Animal Kingdom**:

Pick up a **Discovery Club Passport** for each child in the group.

See how many activities you can complete and how many Discovery Club locations you can explore during your visit. These locations are marked with a red and white **K** on the park map. Make sure to get your Discovery Club Passport stamped at each location.

Decide which location and activity were the most interesting.

50

Match the following animals with the
continents where they live by drawing a line to
connect them.

Animals

Tiger
Gorilla
Komodo Dragon
Raccoon
Eld's Deer
Ball Python
Homing Pigeon
Warthog
Fruit Bat
Striped Skunk
Zebra
Corn Snake
White Rhinoceros
Blackbuck Antelope

Continents

Asia

Africa

N. America

You can observe these animals on **Discovery Island, Kilimanjaro Safaris, Pangani Forest Exploration Trail, Maharajah Jungle Trek, Rafiki's Planet Watch** or at **Camp Minnie-Mickey.**

Did you observe any animals from other continents? Check the **Oasis Exhibits** near the entrance for some interesting possibilities.

51

During your time at the Animal Kingdom, if your group likes thrill rides, try to experience each of the following attractions: **Expedition Everest, Kali River Rapids, Primeval Whirl,** and **DINOSAUR.**

After each attraction, form a family circle and say, "We conquered _____!"

Celebrate with hugs and high fives!

52

At the **Tree of Life:**

Take 15 minutes and write down as many animals as you can find carved on the tree.

Players can find a variety of animals in the root system of the Tree of Life when visiting the paths around it and while walking on the path to the **It's Tough to be a Bug!** attraction.

Playing as a game, the first person to find 20 animals wins.

53

While waiting at **It's Tough to be a Bug!**

Count the number of posters advertising bug-related theater and movie productions.

Work together with adults to figure out and write down the titles of the human versions of these insect productions:

A. *Beauty and the Bees*

_____

B. *A Stinkbug Named Desire*

_____

C. *My Fair Ladybug*

_____

D. *Webside Story*

_____

54

At **Kilimanjaro Safaris:**

a.   Predict the first and last animals you will see on the safari.

b.   Write down the animals you would like to see the most and any you would rather not see.

c.   While waiting and during the safari, say "Hakuna Matata" to Cast Members and your guide. What was their response?

d.   After the safari, write down the names of the rarest animal, the most peaceful animal, and the most exciting animal that you encountered.

55

At **Rafiki's Planet Watch:**

a.   Try to observe some African animals during the **Wildlife Express Train** ride to Rafiki's Planet Watch.

b.   At the **Conservation Station,** observe a veterinary procedure or a live animal demonstration. Which animal(s) did you encounter?

c.   Try to identify some strange sounds you hear in the rain forest exhibit.

d.   Check in on animals around the Animal Kingdom using the camera monitoring system.

e.   At the **Affection Section,** pet (feed and brush, too, if desired) at least three types of animals and try to find a llama. Are there any animals here that you have never seen before? Were the animals all friendly or were some shy?

56

Work together or play a game to be the first to find the unique performance artist called **DiVine**. She is green, leafy, quite tall, and blends in perfectly in the lush green wooded areas at Animal Kingdom.

DiVine is normally found hiding in the woods or walking along the pathways between Asia and Africa. Keep a sharp lookout for this amazing performer.

57

At **Expedition Everest:**

a.   Write down the name of the tour company and the name of the rail service you will be traveling with on your expedition.

_____

_____

b.   Find an outdoor pagoda shrine featuring a statue of a Yeti with various gifts placed around it to honor him. Ring a bell near the shrine to pay tribute to the Yeti.

c.   Find a tent, first aid box, and other equipment used on an expedition to locate the Yeti.

d.   Find the mask of a Yeti on the wall. Find Yeti scat or droppings, footprints, and other evidence said to prove the existence of the Yeti.

e.   What is the name of the legendary animal, said to be related to the Yeti, which lives in North America?

f.   True or False: The artificial mountain at Expedition Everest is taller than any real mountain in Florida.

58

At the **Kali River Rapids:**

a.   Predict who in your group will get the wettest and who will stay the driest. Did anyone get both guesses correct?

b.   In line, find a mahogany panel with animals considered holy in the fictional Kingdom of Anandapur.

c.   Find large sculptures honoring a tiger and a king cobra.

d.   Find the enchanting Painted Pavilion with beautiful paintings of famous stories on the ceiling. See if you can find the panels telling the stories of "The Monkey King" and "The Fearless Lion and Brave Elephant."

e.   Where has the owner of the shop, Mr. Panika, temporarily gone?

f.   Can you find any live animals Mr. Panika keeps as pets?

g.   Find a portrait of the Royal Couple of Anandapur in the Kali River Rapids Expeditions office.

h.   Find the Raft Position Board and see if any rafts are overdue.

i.   After the ride, find the controls with green buttons on the bridge crossing the river. Use them to make the red elephants on shore squirt water bursts on passing rafts.

59

At the **Boneyard** in DinoLand U.S.A:

a.   Find the **Xylobone** fossils set in the wall on the hill near the jeep. What happens when you touch the bones?

b.   Step in the dinosaur footprints to hear some peculiar sounds.

c.   Find some large wooden boxes or crates in the area and try pulling on the handles. What happened?

d.   Which species' fossil bones did you dig up in the Boneyard? Did you find any bones of an animal that was not a dinosaur? Was this animal alive during the age of the dinosaurs?

60

At DINOSAUR:

a. What type of large dinosaur is found in the middle of the waiting area?

b. What is the name of the organization you are secretly helping and which dinosaur does the scientist want you to find?

c. How many years back in time are you traveling? What is the name of this era/period?

d. What scary event do most scientists believe caused the extinction or end of the dinosaurs? Can you name a movie that portrayed a similar event happening in the present day?

e. How many dinosaur skeletons and models can you find outside DINOSAUR?

f. Can you find some large living animals related to the dinosaurs in an outdoor exhibit somewhere near the DINOSAUR attraction?

61

At the end of your visit to **Animal Kingdom**:

a.   Write down your five favorite animals that you encountered in Disney's Animal Kingdom. Explain why they are your favorites.

b.   Discuss which continent has the toughest animals and why. Did everyone agree?

General Waiting in Line Activities

62

Ask 5-10 people in line who their favorite Disney character is. How many had the same favorite Disney character as you?

63

Ask 5-10 people in line where they are visiting from. How many are from other countries? Are there any from your home state? Who lived the closest to your family and where were they from?

64

Out of 20 people in line or walking nearby, count how many are wearing watches. How many are holding cell phones, cameras, or other electronic devices? How many are using their electronic devices vs. how many are talking to others? Find three people holding an object in their hands other than electronic devices.

65

Ask 5-10 people what their favorite Disney movie or song is. How many picked your favorite Disney movie or song? What were the most popular choices for each?

66

Play this game while waiting for a musical or theatrical performance as a good warm-up exercise.

Each player speaks or sings a line from a Disney movie or song. The other players will try and guess the movie or song. The player who gets the most answers correct before the performance begins wins.

The group should thank all the players for their performances.

67

Count how many warning or advisory signs you see for the current ride or attraction you are visiting. Do any of them make you think twice about doing this attraction?

68

Count how many people in line or walking by are eating an ice cream or another sweet treat. Playing as a game, the first to count 10 people wins.

<u>69</u>

Ask 5-10 people what their favorite Disney attraction is. Did anyone pick your favorite?

<u>70</u>

Ask 5-10 people which they prefer: cats or dogs or both equally. What is your vote? Which answer won the vote and how close was it? If they prefer neither, ask them what their favorite type of pet is. Did anyone say they didn't like any pets?

71

Use the autograph pages at the back of the book for this activity. There are several pages for use with multiple characters.

Ask people to write personal autographed messages to Mickey Mouse and/or to your favorite characters on the autograph pages. Also, write your own personal messages and sign them.

When you are finished collecting messages and autographs, find the characters in the park and deliver the notes to them. You can also give the notes to a Cast Member and ask them to pass them to the characters. Another option is to keep the notes as souvenirs.

72

While waiting in line or somewhere else, say "I love Mickey Mouse!" (or your favorite Disney character) three times in a louder than normal voice(no screaming please!). What was the reaction from the people around you? See if anyone responds: "I love Mickey Mouse, too!"

73

Play a game of charades featuring Disney characters and themes. Each player will use hand signals, facial expressions, and body motions to give clues to the other group members as they try to guess a Disney-related answer.

74

Play a game of "I Spy," using a color for smaller children and the first letter of an object for older children.

For example, the first player starts off the game by saying, "I spy with my little eye something that starts with the letter 'R' or something that is the color green."

The player who guesses the object first begins the next game.

75

While waiting, everyone in the group will take a turn giving a compliment:

The thing I like best about my (choose one relative or friend) is:

_____.

If you have more time, play another round where everyone compliments another person in the group.

General Activities in Theme Parks

76

Throughout your day, write down the three best non-Cast Member Disney costumes or outfits you see on visitors. Determine an ultimate winner at the end of the day by group consensus.

77

Play a game to try and find the person in line or walking by wearing the most Disney apparel. The player leading at the time you get to the loading area of the attraction or after 15 minutes of walking around the park wins.

78

Play a game where the first person to see five Disney characters greeting people wins. Increase the number of characters for a longer game. To make it more challenging, choose the specific Disney characters you have to find.

79

Write down the names of the attractions you visit where the attendant Cast Members are not smiling or appear unfriendly. There are only a couple locations in the theme parks where the moods and expressions of the Cast Members intentionally match the gloomy or serious attractions.

<u>80</u>

Work together or play a game to see who can find 3~5 **Hidden Mickeys** in the fastest time at each theme park you visit.

Hidden Mickeys are subtle silhouettes, abstract images, drawings, and shapes revealing Mickey's famous head and ears or his full body.

Hidden Mickeys come in all different sizes and are found in objects and gardens, on buildings, and at attractions throughout the parks.

If you want a little help, ask a Cast Member for some hints on how to find nearby Hidden Mickeys.

81

Find 5-10 visitors wearing professional sports team apparel. To make it more challenging, don't count baseball caps. Was anyone wearing your favorite team's apparel? You can also try this activity with college sports team apparel.

82

Write down the different types of outfits that you see Mickey Mouse wearing as a character and when he is portrayed on various objects throughout the park. Which outfits were the group's favorites?

83

Walk behind a teammate (parent, sibling, or friend) for five minutes without swinging your arms. After completing this exercise, switch positions and walk normally in front of your teammate, while they walk without swinging their arms. Don't walk too fast and don't do this activity if it's too crowded.

84

Find 5-10 people wearing funny shirts with Disney themes and expressions. Which one was your favorite?

85

Find five types of hedges shaped like Disney characters, animals, or objects and write them down. This unique gardening art form is called topiary and is found throughout Walt Disney World.

There are many new and interesting examples of topiary at the **EPCOT International Flower and Garden Festival,** which takes place every spring for a six week period.

86

Find different people outside of your group with brown, black, blonde, strawberry blonde, red, gray, and white hair. See if you can find anyone with hair dyed an unusual color such as green, pink, or purple. The first person to get all the undyed colors wins. If, however, a player spots someone with hair dyed an unusual color, they win immediately.

87

Hold up a piece of paper saying "If you like Mickey Mouse (or your favorite character), give me a high five!" You can also use a fist pump, thumbs up, or other positive hand signal in your message.

See how many positive responses you can get in five minutes.

88

Play a game to be the first to find twins who are dressed alike. Anyone who finds triplets or higher will receive extra congratulations from the group.

89

Find honeymoon couples wearing bride and groom mouse ears. The first player to find five couples during the visit wins.

<u>90</u>

Play a game where players try to find different men with the following facial hair:

a. Mustache
b. Beard
c. Goatee
d. Sideburns

The first player to find a different man with each type of facial hair wins.

91

Find at least three active duty military service members or military veterans wearing uniforms, caps, and/or shirts indicating they served. Thank them for their service to this country.

92

Play a game where each player tries to find five people not wearing sneakers, flip flops, sandals, or crocs.

93

Stare at something ordinary (such as a wall or lamp post) for thirty seconds with your hand shading your eyes. Did anyone start to stare, too, or ask you what you were looking at?

94

Find a Cast Member or visitor with fairy dust or glitter sprinkled on them. Ask them if they have any extra dust to sprinkle on you and your group.

95

Write down the different types of transportation your group has used to get to and around the resorts and theme parks. Which was your favorite? Have the group vote on their favorite and see what is the most popular.

Were there any types of transportation you observed in use that you would like to experience on another visit?

96

Imitate a dancing or singing performer during a street parade or show. Did the performer notice you and wave or smile?

97

Write down the biggest dessert, biggest drink, and biggest meal you have each day and for the entire trip. Were these huge items also your favorites or is big not necessarily the best?

98

Make a check mark on this page every time during the day or hour you hear someone speaking a language other than English. Could you tell what any of the foreign languages were?

99

Play a game where each group member picks a color and counts how many people pass by wearing their selected color. The main color each person is wearing is the only one counted in the game. Play the game for 10 minutes or another set time period. The player who counts the most people wearing their chosen color wins.

Anywhere Activities

100

Have all interested group members make up a dance move based on their favorite Disney characters and have them perform it enthusiastically. After everyone finishes, the group will give a compliment to all participants. Sample compliments: most creative, most enthusiastic, fastest legs, funniest dancer, etc.

101

Softly sing a couple verses of "It's a Small World (After All)," "The Mickey Mouse Club March," "Supercalifragilisticexpialidocious," "Zip-a-Dee-Doo-Dah," or other Disney favorite. Song lyrics are found at the back of the book starting on page 165. Did anyone join in or encourage you?

102

Have all family members guess how many miles your Disney resort or theme park is from your hometown. Don't use any outside help until after everyone guesses! The closest guess wins the game. Did anyone come within 50 miles of the correct answer?

103

Are there any Disney movies that you would change the ending to if you could? How would you change them to improve them in your eyes? Which movies would the rest of the family change and how?

104

Have a discussion with your group about Disney movies and determine by consensus:

a.   What is the saddest scene of them all?

b.   What is the happiest scene of them all?

c.   What is the scariest scene of them all?

d.   What is the funniest scene of them all?

105

At the end of each day, form a circle and say together "Walt and Mickey would be proud of the

_____ family today!"

Give hugs or high fives and celebrate with enthusiasm.

106

Discuss and determine who the scariest Disney villain and the most powerful Disney hero are. Did everyone agree?

107

Have everyone do their best vocal imitation of a Disney character. Vote on who was the closest to the real character.

108

Have everyone in the group make up a fantasy attraction or performance combining at least two Disney attractions from different theme parks. At the end of the discussion, determine which ideas sound the most fun, most conceivable, and most creative.

109

Form your group into a circle. Each player will now guess the person to the right's favorite Disney character, movie, and song.

Each player will then guess the person to the left's least favorite Disney character, movie, and song.

Were there a lot of surprising answers?

Playing as a game, the winning player will have the most correct guesses.

110

Have everyone predict how many family members will have sore feet or blisters at the end of each day. Guess who will have the most blisters, the ugliest blister, and the biggest blister. See who had the best guesses at the end of the day.

111

If you have enough space somewhere outside, perform your favorite state or school song or cheer. Did anyone join in or encourage you? Did anyone disapprove?

112

Make up a family password or catchy phrase each day of your visit. Use it when knocking on family hotel room doors and when greeting family members during your visit.

113

Think of five things in everyday life you would like to use a FASTPASS for if it were possible. Playing as a game, vote on who came up with the best example.

114

Play a game of twenty questions that is Disney-related. One player will think of something in the Disney universe and the others will ask up to twenty yes or no questions to try and determine what or who it is.

The person who guesses the right answer starts the next game.

115

Have a discussion on what type of creature Goofy is: man, dog, man-dog hybrid, or just a one-of-a-kind Goofy. What was the most popular answer?

116

Have a discussion on which five Disney movies or animated features you would want with you for entertainment if you were stranded on a desert island.

Which would you choose if you could only have two?

What if you could only have one movie with you?

117

Discuss and vote on your favorite Disney Princesses and Heroines from 1~5.

Discuss and vote on your favorite Disney Princes and Heroes from 1~5.

Discuss and vote on your favorite Disney fantasy vehicles, gadgets, or inventions from 1~5.

118

Create your own customized Disney saying similar to the classic "Have a Magical Day!"

Try it out and see if others like it.

AUTOGRAPH PAGES

Fan Messages and Autographs for Disney Characters

For use with #71 in Games and Activities

Character_____

Fan Messages and Autographs:

Character_____

Fan Messages and Autographs:

Character_____

Fan Messages and Autographs:

Character_____

Fan Messages and Autographs:

Character_____

Fan Messages and Autographs:

Character_____

Fan Messages and Autographs:

Character_____

Fan Messages and Autographs:

Character_____

Fan Messages and Autographs:

My Autographs from
Disney Characters

Autographs

Autographs

Autographs

Autographs

Autographs

Autographs

Autographs

DISNEY MEMORIES

Draw Your Favorite Disney Characters

Drawings

Drawings

Drawings

Drawings

Drawings

My Favorite Attractions

<u>Day One</u>

1.

2.

3.

<u>Day Two</u>

1.

2.

3.

<u>Day Three</u>

1.

2.

3.

<u>Day Four</u>

1.

2.

3.

<u>Day Five</u>

1.

2.

3.

<u>Day Six</u>

1.

2.

3.

<u>Day Seven</u>

1.

2.

3.

<u>Best of Trip</u>

1.

2.

3.

My Favorite Attractions

Day One

1.

2.

3.

Day Two

1.

2.

3.

Day Three

1.

2.

3.

Day Four

1.

2.

3.

Day Five

1.

2.

3.

Day Six

1.

2.

3.

Day Seven

1.

2.

3.

Best of Trip

1.

2.

3.

My Favorite Attractions

<u>Day One</u>

1.

2.

3.

<u>Day Two</u>

1.

2.

3.

<u>Day Three</u>

1.

2.

3.

<u>Day Four</u>

1.

2.

3.

<u>Day Five</u>

1.

2.

3.

<u>Day Six</u>

1.

2.

3.

<u>Day Seven</u>

1.

2.

3.

<u>Best of Trip</u>

1.

2.

3.

My Favorite Attractions

Day One

1.

2.

3.

Day Two

1.

2.

3.

Day Three

1.

2.

3.

Day Four

1.

2.

3.

Day Five

1.

2.

3.

Day Six

1.

2.

3.

Day Seven

1.

2.

3.

Best of Trip

1.

2.

3.

My Favorite Disney Parades and Fireworks Shows

My Favorite Disney Parades and Fireworks Shows

My Favorite Disney Parades and Fireworks Shows

My Favorite Disney Parades and Fireworks Shows

My Favorite Disney Memories

My Favorite Disney Memories

My Favorite Disney Memories

My Favorite Disney Memories

My Favorite Disney Photos

My Favorite Disney Photos

My Favorite Disney Photos

My Favorite Disney Photos

SONG LYRICS

"It's a Small World (After All)"

Lyrics

It's a world of laughter, a world of tears
it's a world of hopes, it's a world of fear
there's so much that we share
that it's time we're aware
it's a small world after all

It's a small world after all
it's a small world after all
it's a small world after all
it's a small, small world

There is just one moon and one golden sun
And a smile means friendship to everyone

Though the mountains divide
And the oceans are wide
It's a small, small world

It's a small world after all
it's a small world after all
it's a small world after all
it's a small, small world

The Mickey Mouse Club March

Lyrics

Who's the leader of the club
That's made for you and me
M-I-C-K-E-Y M-O-U-S-E
Hey! there, Hi! there, Ho! there
You're as welcome as can be
M-I-C-K-E-Y M-O-U-S-E

Mickey Mouse! Mickey Mouse!

Forever let us hold our banner
High! High! High! High!

Come along and sing a song
And join the jamboree!
M-I-C-K-E-Y M-O-U-S-E

Mickey Mouse club
We'll have fun
We'll be new faces
High! High! High! High!
We'll do things and
We'll go places
All around the world
We'll go marching

Who's the leader of the club
That's made for you and me
M-I-C-K-E-Y M-O-U-S-E
Hey! there, Hi! there, Ho! there
You're as welcome as can be
M-I-C-K-E-Y M-O-U-S-E

Mickey Mouse! Mickey Mouse!

Forever let us hold our banner
High! High! High! High!

Come along and sing a song
And join the jamboree!
M-I-C-K-E-Y M-O-U-S-E

Supercalifragilisticexpialidocious

Lyrics

Mary Poppins:
It's…
Supercalifragilisticexpialidocious!
Even though the sound of it
Is something quite atrocious
If you say it loud enough
You'll always sound precocious

All:
Supercalifragilisticexpialidocious!
Um diddle diddle diddle um diddle ay
Um diddle diddle diddle um diddle ay!

Bert:
Because I was afraid to speak
When I was just a lad
My father gave me nose a tweak
And told me I was bad
But then one day I learned a word
That saved me achin' nose

Bert, Mary Poppins and Chorus:
The biggest word I ever heard
And this is how it goes: Oh!

Supercalifragilisticexpialidocious!
Even though the sound of it
Is something quite atrocious

If you say it loud enough
You'll always sound precocious
Supercalifragilisticexpialidocious!
Um diddle diddle diddle um diddle ay
Um diddle diddle diddle um diddle ay!

Mary Poppins:
He traveled all around the world
And everywhere he went
He'd use his word and all would say
"There goes a clever gent"

Bert:
When Dukes and maharajas
Pass the time of day with me
I say me special word and then
They ask me out to tea

Bert, Mary Poppins and Chorus:
Oh..
Supercalifragilisticexpialidocious!
Even though the sound of it
Is something quite atrocious
If you say it loud enough
You'll always sound precocious
Supercalifragilisticexpialidocious!
Um diddle diddle diddle um diddle ay
Um diddle diddle diddle um diddle ay!

Mary Poppins:
So when the cat has got your tongue
There's no need for dismay
Just summon up this word
And then you've got a lot to say

But better use it carefully
Or it could change your life

The Perlie:
One night I said it to me girl
And now me girl's my wife!

All:
She's supercalifragilisticexpialidocious!
Supercalifragilisticexpialidocious
Supercalifragilisticexpialidocious
Supercalifragilisticexpialidocious

Zip-a-Dee-Doo-Dah

Lyrics

Zip a dee doo dah zip a dee a
My oh my, what a wonderful day
Plenty of sunshine heading my way

Zip a dee doo dah zip a dee a
Mister Bluebird on my shoulder
It's the truth it's actual everything is satisfactual

Zip a dee doo dah zip a dee a
Wonderful feeling wonderful day

Zip a dee doo dah zip a dee a
Wonderful feeling wonderful day
Plenty of sunshine heading my way

Zip a dee doo dah zip a dee a
My oh my, what a wonderful day
Zip a dee doo dah zip a dee a
Plenty of sunshine heading my way

Mister Bluebird on my shoulder
It's the truth it's actual everything is satisfactual
Zip a dee doo dah zip a dee a
Wonderful feeling wonderful day

Zip a dee doo
Zip a dee doo

Zip a dee doo dah
Zip a dee doo dah

Zip a dee doo dah
Zip zip zip a dee a
Zip a dee doo dah

HELPFUL DISNEY TIPS

Planning and Timing Your Visit

➢ The least crowded and most affordable times to visit Walt Disney World correspond to non-school vacation periods and non-holiday times. The least crowded approximate time periods are: mid-January to mid-February, mid-July to mid-November, and after Thanksgiving to mid-December. Avoid any holiday or specially-themed weekends during those times.

➢ Every day one theme park opens an hour early or remains open up to two extra hours for guests staying at Walt Disney World resorts. This program is called **Extra Magic Hours**. Check these times carefully to more efficiently plan your visit. The **Disney Water Parks** also sometimes offer this feature.

➢ Most visitors to Disney World go to the Magic Kingdom on the first or second day of their visit. During holiday weeks especially, plan to visit the Magic Kingdom in the middle or end of the week to avoid the biggest crowds.

➢ Some of the stores and restaurants in the parks stay open up to 30-60 minutes after the parks' official closing times. Take advantage of this if you want to avoid the worst of the crowds heading for the exits.

➢ There are many sources offering specific strategies on how to best beat the lines at Disney, but the following general tips will help. Most importantly, arrive early and plan to visit the most popular attractions first. Be at the entrance to the theme parks at least thirty minutes before they officially open. When the ropes drop, go immediately to the most popular rides that are the farthest away. Pick up a **FASTPASS** at one attraction on the way and then visit the next popular attractions.

➢ Try to visit the most popular attractions as much as possible in the morning and then go back to your hotel/resort during the mid-afternoon to avoid the most crowded time at the parks. Your family can have a relaxing lunch, take a nap, swim at the pool, and then return refreshed to the parks for the late afternoon and evening. If it's not possible to go back to your hotel, keep visiting attractions while the crowds are in the restaurants during the lunch rush between 12 PM-1:30 PM. After the rush, you can then eat lunch at less crowded facilities. Bringing small snacks and drinks with you will help you carry out this plan.

➢ If you are standing in line for an attraction at the park's official closing time, you will be allowed to get on the ride.

➢ As long as you don't mind temporarily splitting up your group, take advantage of the **Single Rider** lines available at most thrill rides. You will get on popular attractions much faster using this option.

Adults traveling with small children or others unable or unwilling to go on some of the thrill rides, can take advantage of the **Rider Switch Program.** Using this feature you can avoid waiting in lines twice for the same attraction. The program works by allowing an adult to ride with interested family members, while another adult waits with non-riding children or other family members in a designated area. When the first adult returns from the ride, they can switch places with the other adult, who is then able to experience the attraction without waiting in line again.

Celebrating a Special Occasion at Disney

➢   If someone in your party is celebrating a first visit to Disney, birthday, anniversary, honeymoon, graduation, or other special event, make sure to visit the **Guest Services Office** upon entering any of the theme parks. At the office you will receive some decorative pins or buttons indicating your elite status. These decorations will result in some special treatment and attention from Cast Members throughout your visit.

➢   Guests staying at Disney Resorts can arrange for a special wake-up call or birthday greetings from a Disney character. Contact resort staff to set this up during your visit.

➢   Veterans and active duty military personnel are especially invited to the moving **Flag Retreat** ceremony. This patriotic event takes place daily at 5 PM at the Town Square in the Magic Kingdom. One veteran is randomly selected as a special guest participant in the event and is honored with a certificate, pin, and photos.

Specific Tips for the Magic Kingdom

➤ In the Magic Kingdom, go to the post office in the **City Hall** building and ask for a special Main Street, U.S.A.-Magic Kingdom postmark for your outgoing mail.

➤ About 15 minutes prior to the official opening time, visitors can experience the **Magic Kingdom Welcome Show** where the Mayor of Main Street, U.S.A., welcomes guests to the park in grand style. The ceremony features a song and dance performance from some colorfully dressed townspeople. A few minutes later, a steam train locomotive brings all the Disney characters, led by Mickey Mouse, to the entrance of the Magic Kingdom to officially open the park.

➤ Another benefit to arriving at the Magic Kingdom early is the slim chance of being picked to be the **Grand Marshalls** of the main afternoon parade. Cast Members monitor Main Street in the early morning looking for a fun, enthusiastic couple or family. Some say matching shirts or outfits will help your chances, but there is no widely accepted successful formula. The chosen group gets the honor of riding in the first antique car leading the parade.

➤ If your family needs a break from all the high-paced stimulation at the park, try out the **Tomorrowland Transit Authority People Mover**. This moving tram ride whisks you on a comfortable behind-the-scenes tour of Tomorrowland. Another relaxing ride is **Walt Disney's Carousel of Progress**. This slow moving Audio-Animatronics stage show features a revolving theater. The program follows the progress of technology from the beginning of the 20th Century to today through the eyes of a typical American family. This attraction was originally created by Walt Disney for the New York's World Fair in 1964-65.

➢ Among the many different character meal opportunities throughout Disney World, your family can eat a meal at **Cinderella Castle** for breakfast, lunch, or dinner. When contacting Disney, ask for a reservation at **Cinderella's Royal Table**.

➢ Every guest staying at a Disney resort is automatically entered into a drawing to stay overnight in **Cinderella's Suite** in the castle. If you win, the **Disney Dream Squad** will visit your hotel room and give you and your group VIP treatment throughout the day culminating in an amazing night's stay in the castle.

➢ The nightly **Main Street Electrical Parade** features a dazzling array of colorfully lighted floats led by Tinker Bell and her glowing magic wand. Highlights include half a million blinking lights synchronized with inspiring music, dancing patriotic performers and Disney characters, and a bald eagle made out of brilliant golden lights. If there are two performances, the later show will be less crowded.

➢ For the perfect ending to your visit to the Magic Kingdom, make sure to experience the **Wishes Nighttime Spectacular** fireworks show. Keep a sharp eye out at the beginning to see the breathtaking sight of Tinker Bell's flight from Cinderella Castle to Tomorrowland. Stand somewhere in the Cinderella Castle forecourt or on one of the surrounding bridges for an excellent view of the show. Stake out your viewing spot at least thirty minutes before the show.

➤ There is an entertaining visual show projected onto the front of Cinderella Castle called **Celebrate the Magic** that takes place just before Wishes. Tinker Bell leads a show that features a montage of classic scenes from Disney films, amazing animated sequences, soaring music, and other stunning special effects. During holiday times the show also mixes in seasonally-themed sequences.

➤ About 3o minutes after the official park closing time, you can experience the **Kiss Goodnight**. At this time, Cinderella Castle is bathed in colorful, twinkling lights accompanied by music and an announcement thanking you for visiting. It concludes with Mickey's voice bidding you a fond farewell.

➤ Fans of Tinker Bell and all the Disney fairies can meet them throughout the day in the Magic Kingdom at **Tinker Bell's Magical Nook** in Adventureland.

➤ For a special view of the Wishes Nighttime Spectacular fireworks show at the Magic Kingdom, take the **Pirates & Pals Fireworks Voyage** leaving nightly from near the **Contemporary Resort**. Captain Hook and Mr. Smee will see your group off at the docks. Your pirate captain Patch will entertain everyone with songs and games during the moonlit cruise of the **Seven Seas Lagoon**. After you enjoy the special view of the fireworks show, Patch will tell the exciting tale of Peter Pan. A special guest will welcome your group back to the docks to end your voyage in style.

➤ **Bibbidi Bobbidi Boutique** is a special place at Cinderella Castle in the Magic Kingdom and at **Downtown Disney**, where little girls are transformed into magical princesses and fairies. A Fairy Godmother also makes regular appearances in the nearby Castle Courtyard.

➤ **Captain Jack Sparrow's Pirate Tutorial** takes place near the **Pirates of the Caribbean** in the Magic Kingdom. Attendees can learn how to fight with a sword and act like a pirate.

➤ Adults and children can undertake a new interactive quest in the Magic Kingdom called **A Pirate's Adventure: Treasures of the Seven Seas.** Participants take on the role of pirates who have to help Captain Jack Sparrow save the fate of piracy in the Caribbean. Players use treasure maps, magic talismans, and Captain Sparrow's magic compass to collect clues and treasures on five different pirate raids throughout **Adventureland**.

➤ Adults and children can play an interactive role game called **Sorcerers of the Magic Kingdom**. Participants will help the legendary wizard Merlin reassemble the Crystal of the Magic Kingdom which has been broken into four shards. The pieces are hidden in different locations throughout the park. Players will use Merlin's Mystical Map and a Sorcerer Key Card to solve clues and find the shards. They will also have to fight off evil sorcerers and villains using Spell Cards. Begin your adventure at the **Firehouse** on Main Street, U.S.A., or behind the **Ye Olde Christmas Shoppe** in Liberty Square.

Specific Tips for EPCOT

➢ The **EPCOT International Flower and Garden Festival** takes place every spring for a six-week period. Visitors will enjoy amazing topiary displays, illuminated gardens, a butterfly house and gardens, unique children's play areas, and special musical performances.

➢ Don't miss **IllumiNations: Reflections of Earth**, a vividly entertaining fireworks and laser light show featuring a spherical video display system and the Inferno Barge, which shoots balls of fire 60 feet into the air. The show is accompanied by music and narration and takes place around the official park closing time-normally at 9 PM. Find a spot with a good view of the **World Showcase Lagoon** at least 15-30 minutes early to best enjoy the show.

➢ The **EPCOT International Food & Wine Festival** takes place every fall for six weeks. The festival features cuisine and wine from around the world for dining and purchase. Special events include a wide variety of tastings, celebrity chef presentations, and lessons on food and wine pairings and preparation.

➤ Kids will enjoy the interactive scavenger hunt game **Disney Phineas and Ferb: Agent P's World Showcase Adventure**. Players use a special electronic handheld device or F.O.N.E. to find clues at country pavilions to help Agent P, aka Perry the Platypus, thwart the diabolical plans of Dr. Doofenshmirtz. Two to four agents of any age can share the F.ON.E. to carry out a variety of missions that last between 30-45 minutes. Visit a recruitment center at Odyssey Bridge, the Norway or Italy Pavilions, or near the International gateway to pick up a F.O.N.E. to begin your quest to save the world.

➤ Each World Showcase Pavilion has a **Kidcot Fun Stop** where pre-school children can conduct some interesting activities and collect stamps and stickers with a Cast Member native to the country. They will also receive a cardboard cutout of Duffy the Disney Bear, Mickey Mouse's Teddy Bear, to color at each stop.

Specific Tips for Hollywood Studios

➤ Check out the street performances by the **Citizens of Hollywood**. This group is an improvisational acting troupe who interact with the audience during highly entertaining shows. They perform regularly on Hollywood Boulevard.

➢ Star Wars fans should take advantage of the **Jedi Training Academy** near Echo Lake. Children ages 4-12 don brown Padawan robes and learn how to use lightsabers and the Force to battle the Darkside of the Force. Report to the line outside the ABC Sound Studio as soon as the park opens to reserve your training spot. Space is limited so get to the line quickly.

➢ Don't miss the nighttime spectacular show **Fantasmic!** This amazing event features fireworks, live actors and Disney characters, animatronic beasts, boats, soaring music, and water and laser light effects. Depending upon the season, plan to be there 1-2 hours before the scheduled start of the show to get a good seat. A useful strategy is to have one person hold a place in line, while the other group members get food or explore the park. If they offer two shows that evening, attend the later show to avoid the larger crowd. Another option is to use the **Fantasmic Dining Package**, which combines a dinner reservation at a park restaurant with guaranteed priority seating at the show.

Specific Tips for Animal Kingdom

➢ Avoid some of the crowd at the park opening by entering through the **Rain Forest Café.**

➢ There is a special opening ceremony featuring Mickey, Minnie, Goofy, and Pluto. This show takes place about 15 minutes prior to the official opening time.

➢ The **Camp Minnie-Mickey** area is a relatively uncrowded location to meet your favorite Disney characters. Visit the indoor **Adventurer's Outpost** on Discovery Island to meet Minnie and Mickey.

➢ Adults and children can participate in a new interactive experience at Animal Kingdom called **Wilderness Explorers Adventure Organization** featuring characters from the movie *Up*. Participants will use special field guides to complete challenges throughout the park to earn up to 30 badges and become Wilderness Explorers.

➢ Visit the **Animal Kingdom Lodge**, a resort which feels like an African village. It is surrounded on three sides by specially-designed savannahs with dozens of African animals, including giraffes and zebras. Some resort guests can observe the exotic wildlife from their room balconies, while visitors can enjoy this unique experience from designated viewing locations.

Fun Activities Outside the Theme Parks

➢ For some old-fashioned family fun, check out **Chip 'N Dale's Campfire Sing-A-Long** nightly at 7 PM or 8 PM depending upon the time of year. This event takes place at the **Campsites at Disney's Fort Wilderness Resort**. Guests can also toast marshmallows (bring your own or purchase them there) and watch a classic Disney movie or cartoon outside after the sing-along.

The Fort Wilderness Resort also offers horseback riding and wagon rides at the **Tri-Circle-D Ranch**. The resort also features the **Hoop-Dee-Doo Musical Revue**. These dinner shows combine frontier-style singing, dancing, and vaudeville comedy with hearty country food.

The resort also offers **Mickey's Backyard BBQ** at their open air pavilion. This dinner show features a barbecue feast and hoedown with a live country western band, cowboy rope tricks, and line dancing with your favorite Disney characters. These popular shows are seasonal and offered on a limited basis.

➤ A day at a **Disney Water Park** will work nicely for visitors looking for a cool break from the hot days of touring the theme parks. Disney offers a variety of water activities at their two water parks: **Typhoon Lagoon** and **Blizzard Beach**.

Typhoon Lagoon has a giant wave pool, waterslides of all shapes and sizes, a children's play area, and a coral reef where you can snorkel among marine life. The **Crush 'N Gusher** water coaster is only for true thrill seekers. They also offer private surfing lessons and a **Private Surf and Party** event for up to 25 people who want to learn to surf in the wave pool. Surfing is available before the park opens.

Blizzard Beach also offers a wave pool, raft rides, and challenging waterslides, including **Mount Gushmore**, one of the world's tallest and fastest.

➤ Parasailing is available throughout the day in **Bay Lake** at the Magic Kingdom. Make reservations at

Sammy Duvall's Watersports Centre at the **Contemporary Resort**. Riders can fly solo or tandem with a partner and will enjoy fantastic bird's-eye views of the Magic Kingdom.

➢ The **Electrical Water Pageant** is a unique nighttime parade on water that takes place on Bay Lake and the Seven Seas Lagoon. Boats decorated with brilliantly lighted designs of mythical and real sea creatures cruise on the water accompanied by electronic music. The parade culminates with a float featuring America flags and blinking stars and a medley of patriotic music. You can view the show from any of the Disney resorts on the water and at the entrance to the Magic Kingdom.

➢ Miniature Golf fans can try out two grand courses: the **Fantasia Gardens Miniature Golf Course** located near the Swan and Dolphin resorts and the **Winter Summerland Miniature Golf Course** near Blizzard Beach.

➢ The area near the **BoardWalk Inn** resort features midway carnival games during the day, rentable bikes built for 4, an arcade, and evening street performers. There is also an ESPN Club, as well as many restaurants and clubs featuring dancing, dueling pianos, and other live entertainment.

➢ **Downtown Disney** offers a movie theater, bowling lanes, the **DisneyQuest Indoor Interactive Theme Park**, the **Bibbidi Bobbidi Botique** (princess transformation area) at the world's largest **Disney Store,** restaurants, clubs and a huge variety of stores. The Indoor Interactive Theme Park features a variety of interactive games in virtual worlds including **Cyber Space Mountain**, where you create your own roller coaster track and ride on it in a simulator.

➤   At Downtown Disney you can take in a spectacular view of Disney World from 400 feet up in the air in the world's largest tethered helium balloon. The attraction is called **Characters in Flight** as the balloon is covered with drawings of beloved flying Disney characters. You can ascend into the heavens daily until midnight.

➤   Downtown Disney hosts **Car Masters Weekend** normally on a weekend in June. This event features classic and exotic cars, meet and greets with automotive and racing celebrities and Disney characters, and opportunities to race high-performance karts.

➤   Guests can pamper themselves at **Senses,** a full-service spa located at **Disney's Grand Floridian Resort.** This spa and health club is presented in a Victorian-themed setting and is designed to relax and rejuvenate. They offer body treatments, therapies, and massages, as well as steam rooms and whirlpools.

➤   Experience the thrill of driving or riding in an authentic NASCAR race car by participating in the **Richard Petty Driving Experience** at the **Walt Disney**

World Speedway. Participants can drive at speeds up to 120 mph on the mile-long oval track or ride along with a professional instructor who will push the car up to 140 mph.

VIP and Behind-the-Scenes Tours

➤ Disney offers a behind the scenes look at the Magic Kingdom, including a visit to the famous underground tunnels known as "Utilidors," through their **Keys to the Kingdom Tour.** They also offer a **Backstage Magic Tour**, which gives you an all day behind the scenes look at the workings of attractions at all four theme parks and more.

➤ Disney also provides **VIP Tour Services** with a personal VIP Tour Guide leading your group of up to 10 people through any or all of the theme parks. The VIP service will arrange your customized itinerary and provide your group with VIP access to attractions, parades, shows, and special events.

➤ Railroad enthusiasts should experience **Disney's The Magic Behind Our Steam Trains Tour**, a 3 hour tour offered every morning. The tour provides backstage access to the roundhouse, where the park's steam engines are maintained, interaction with the Cast Members who take care of and operate the trains, insight into Walt Disney's passion for steam trains, and a special ride around the park in a fully restored antique freight train.

➤ EPCOT offers the **EPCOT DiveQuest** for any SCUBA-certified visitor 10 years of age or older. Participants will dive into the 5.7 million gallon saltwater aquarium known as the **Caribbean Coral Reef** and swim with over 6,000 types of marine animals.

➤ Visitors who aren't SCUBA-certified can do a similar snorkeling excursion in the aquarium in a program called the **EPCOT Seas Aqua Tour**. Both of these activities also include a backstage tour of the infrastructure that supports this massive underwater exhibit.

➤ EPCOT also offers a Dolphin encounter for visitors age 13 and older called **Disney's Dolphins in Depth**. Guests interact with the dolphins in the water and observe research and training sessions conducted by Disney's marine mammal specialists.

➤ Animal Kingdom offers a **Backstage Safari**, which features a look at the facilities and personnel needed to feed and care for the animals at the park. The 3-hr program concludes with a private Kilimanjaro Safaris outing.

➤ Animal Kingdom also offers the **Wild Africa Trek**, designed for tweens and up. On this 3-hr. safari, a guide takes the group on a private walking and riding tour of the **Harambe Reserve**. One highlight is an invigorating walk across a teetering rope bridge. Participants are secured only by a safety harness as they walk just 10 feet above huge hippos and crocodiles.

➤ The Animal Kingdom's **Wild by Design** tour is a 3-hr walking program, focusing on the onstage areas of the park. Guests will learn about the amazing efforts made by Disney Imagineers in designing the park's authentic attractions and will also interact with skilled animal handlers.

Holidays at Walt Disney World

Walt Disney World offers a wide variety of seasonally-themed decorations and events.

➤ The Magic Kingdom celebrates the Christmas season with a huge Christmas tree and lights, ornaments, wreaths, garlands, and other holiday decorations adorning the entire park. There is a nightly **Cinderella's Holiday Wish Stage Show** with festive performances. After the show, Cinderella Castle is brilliantly lit up with an impressive array of more than 200,000 twinkling **Dream Lights**. Visitors can meet Santa Claus and Mrs. Claus during the day at the **Tour Guide Gardens** near **City Hall**.

➤ Special tickets are needed for **Mickey's Very Merry Christmas Party**, which occurs on select evenings in November and December from 7 PM-12 AM. Ticket holders can enter the park as early as 4 PM. Highlights of the party include artificial snow falling on Main Street, complimentary cookies and hot cocoa, and **Mickey's Once Upon a Christmastime Parade**. The parade features Disney characters, gingerbread men, wooden soldiers, and Santa Claus. The parade runs twice nightly. The later parade is normally less crowded. The evening concludes with a holiday version of the Wishes fireworks event.

➤ EPCOT features storytellers at the international pavilions explaining the different ways their countries celebrate the holiday. The show **Joyfull** features regular Gospel performances at the **Fountain Stage**.

➤ The most popular holiday event at EPCOT is the **Candlelight Processional,** a performance held at the **America Gardens Theatre**. This attractive venue is located on the **World Showcase Lagoon** across from the **American Adventure Pavilion**. This inspirational event features a mass choir, a full orchestra, and a celebrity narrator relating the Christmas Story. There are three performances nightly. It is highly recommended to reserve a dinner package at one of the pavilion restaurants to guarantee seating at this popular event. The evening at EPCOT concludes with a holiday-themed **IllumiNations** laser, light and fireworks show.

➤ Animal Kingdom features an animal-themed Christmas tree and many trees at Camp Minnie-Mickey trimmed with Disney decorations. Goofy dresses up as Santa at **Santa Goofy's Wild Wonderland** making for some fun photos. **Mickey's Jingle Jungle Parade** combines holiday decorations and music with a safari setting.

➤ Hollywood Studios celebrates the Christmas season with traditional holiday decorations throughout the park. The highlight is the nightly **Osborne Family Spectacle of Dancing Lights** on the Streets of America. This popular performance features brilliantly colored and flashing LED lights that cover the streets and buildings. The blinking lights are synchronized with the beat of inspirational holiday music to the delight of visitors.

➤ The Magic Kingdom features **Mickey's Not-So-Scary Halloween Party** on select nights in September and October. This party requires a special ticket. The event encourages visitors to dress up in their favorite Halloween costumes and come prepared to trick-or-treat and meet with their favorite Disney characters in their Halloween costumes. Highlights include a lively parade and the **Disney Villains Dance Mix and Mingle**. This event features some of Disney's scariest villains singing and dancing in front of Cinderella Castle and then mingling with visitors.

➤ At **Mickey's "Boo-to-You" Parade**, the festivities start with the ghostly appearance of the Headless Horseman. The parade floats feature Disney characters in Halloween costumes. If two parade times are offered, the later event is normally less crowded.

➤ The finale of the Halloween party is the fireworks and music show called **Happy HalloWishes** featuring haunting pyrotechnic effects, creepy music, and appearances from famous Disney villains such as Cruella de Vil, Oogie Boogie, Maleficent, Jafar, and

Ursula. Cinderella Castle is bathed in eerie colors during this exhilarating Halloween experience.

Answer Key for Selected Activities

1   **b.** The train is delayed because of a bear on the track. **c.** This special message is from Walt Disney's speech at the opening day of Disneyland in 1955.

2.   **a.** Goofy will sometimes laugh and talk to you when you sit next to him. **c.** Roy Disney was a crucial partner who continued his brother's ambitious mission after his death. **f.** Mickey Mouse has bigger feet and ears. Walt Disney is wearing rings on both fingers. The Irish Claddagh wedding ring on his right ring finger resembles a silhouette of Mickey's famous ears.
g. There are seven statues with nine Disney characters represented: Chip 'N Dale, Dumbo the Flying Elephant, Goofy, Minnie Mouse, Br'er Rabbit, Pluto, and Pinocchio with Jiminy Cricket. Different statues of Disney characters in costumes also appear in this area to celebrate Halloween.

3.   The Lands are all in their own distinct areas marked by different colored pavement and different music and decorations.

5.   **a.** The flag of Switzerland flies outside the Swiss Family Treehouse. **b.** The camel has two humps.

6.   **a.** The employee of the month's name is E.L. O'Fevre (Yellow Fever). **c.** The free kittens with their pretty stripes are tiger cubs. **d.** Crew mess items

include Barbecued Three-Toed Skink and Fricassee of Giant Stag Beetle. Sounds delicious!

7.   **b.** An approximate number is fine as the number will depend on your location in line and your seat location during the attraction.   **c.** The chess game is at a stalemate position, where neither player can win. **e.** "Dead men tell no tales!"   **f.** The painted pirate footprints feature boot prints next to circular impressions. The message to exit in this direction includes any pirate who might have a wooden leg.

8c.   There are three main Br'er characters: Br'er Rabbit, Br'er Fox and Br'er Bear. Br'er is short for "Brother."

9.   **a.** A red sign on the wall near the entrance tells miners that they are required to stay at the Big Thunder Boarding House. It then states: "Meal provided daily. Baths weekly."   **c.** When viewing the subterrascope, one scene reveals a woman taking some gold nuggets for herself.   **d.** You can find this crate on top of some barrels near the exit to the attraction.

10.   **a.** The Country Bears made these claw marks. **b.** There are 13 lanterns on the tree representing the 13 colonies during the American Revolutionary War. The two lanterns represent the two lanterns lit in the tower of the Old North Church in Boston on the night of April 18, 1775, at the start of the war. These lanterns signaled to riders, including Paul Revere, how British troops would be traveling to Concord to seize and destroy rebel weapons and ammunition. The signal sent by the lanterns would be "One if by land, two if by

sea." **c.** There is a crack in the bell. It is located in Philadelphia.

11.   Some of the tombstones and crypts at the Haunted Mansion pay tribute to the Imagineers and artists that made it possible, while others are related to characters and stories in Haunted Mansion lore.
b. Carefully read the plates with the inscriptions and note the symbols, which reveal the method of murder the characters used. Start by reading the clue in Uncle Jacob's inscription, which reveals that he was killed by poison. Then go to Bertie's memorial, which has a poison bottle and reveals that he was shot. Next find the revolver on Aunt Florence's memorial, which reveals she shot Bertie. The inscription tells you that she was killed while feeding her canary. The Twins memorial reveals they killed Aunt Florence while she was feeding her canary and were later killed by blows to the head. Aunt Maude's memorial reveals she killed the twins with a hammer and then died from a fire in her bed. If you look in her hair bun you will see the matches that ignited accidentally while she was sleeping.   **c.** The Composer's Crypt has normal instruments on the front of it that play when you touch them. The pipe organ plays scary notes and sometimes blows air and water when you touch the keys. The raven, who appears in the attraction, is perched on the pipes of the organ. On the opposite side of the tomb, you can touch instruments from the afterlife to make them play and you can hear the screech of a one-eyed cat when you touch it.   **d.** Master Gracey's tombstone sometimes has a flower on top of it depending upon the Cast Members. He is a popular character in Haunted

Mansion lore. **e.** If you put your fingers over the holes in the Sea Captain's Crypt, water will squirt out of other holes. At certain intervals you will hear the captain singing and bubbles will come out of the crypt. The Poetess asks for your help to complete her poems. **f.** The bride's ring is found to the right of the Sea Captain's Crypt embedded in the concrete near the wall. There are different versions of who the bride was and what happened to her. Some stories say the ring belonged to one of Master Gracey's wives who met an unusual and untimely death. One version says she playfully hid in a trunk from Master Gracey on their wedding night, but couldn't escape it after she closed the lid and suffocated. Other versions suggest she was murdered. One popular account says the ring got where it is now on their wedding day. The happy couple was riding in a horse-drawn carriage when the horse got spooked by something, reared up and violently shook the carriage. The bride lost the ring and the horse stomped it into the concrete. Ask a Cast Member for their favorite version of the story. **g.** At the Library Crypt pushing the books into the bookshelf causes other books to pop out. There is a secret message conveyed by symbols on some of the books. This Cryptogram is difficult to solve without some help. The secret message (it is one long sentence of four phrases that rhyme) starts at the top row center panel of the library then proceeds to the second row far left panel and continues left to right from there ending in the bottom row far right panel. Each symbol represents one of the 26 letters in the alphabet. **SPOILER ALERT**-The first five sets of symbols starting in the top row center say "*Welcome home you foolish mortal.*" Try to solve the whole message with this information when you have sufficient time. **i.** Madame Leota's eyes open and look around intermittently. **j.** The Many Adventures of Winnie the Pooh attraction replaced Mr. Toad's Wild Ride.

12.   **a.** Snow White. The Mirror on the Wall. **b.** A pumpkin and mice. **c.** There are seven dwarfs named Doc, Sneezy, Sleepy, Grumpy, Bashful, Happy and Dopey-who doesn't have a beard. **d.** Her real name was Ella, but her stepfamily mockingly called her Cinderella because she was often covered in cinders and ashes from cleaning the fireplace. **e.** A poisoned apple. **f.** Willie the Giant is a character in the *Mickey in the Beanstalk* segment of *Fun and Fancy Free*. There is a large painting of him trying to reach into the store.

14.   **a.** The large crocodile above the FastPass sign is known as Tick-Tock. In the story, Peter Pan cut off Captain Hook's hand and fed it to Tick-Tock, who found it delicious. Since then he has always followed Hook hoping to eat the rest of him. Luckily for Captain Hook, the crocodile also swallowed an alarm clock at some point. The clock's constant ticking always warns Hook that Tick-Tock is nearby. **c.** Tinker Bell's pixie dust or fairy dust. **d.** Peter Pan lives in Neverland with his faithful band known as the Lost Boys. **e.** London

15.   **a.** There are more brass instruments. **c.** *Fantasia*

16.   **a.** 90 horses. **c.** Merry-go-round

17.   **a.** An approximate number is fine as some are hidden more than others.   **b.** Pooh's residence is in Mr. Sanders tree. This tree was previously found nearby in a Pooh-themed playground where the 20,000 Leagues Under the Sea attraction once stood. This wooden carving of the *Nautilus* submarine pays tribute to this attraction.   **c.** When you touch the storybook page, voices of the characters will answer you.   **g.** This painting pays tribute to the attraction that previously stood here called Mr. Toad's Wild Ride. The painting represents Mr. Toad handing the deed of the location over to Owl to symbolize the change in attractions. **h.** Pooh spells honey "hunny." There are other examples of misspelled words throughout the attraction.   **i.** When Pooh is annoyed he will often say, "Oh, bother!"

19.   There are three castles in the Magic Kingdom belonging to Cinderella, Beast, and Prince Eric.

20.   **a.** Gaston and LaFou from *Beauty and the Beast.* **b.** You will find many similar looking gargoyles on a bridge. There are other gargoyles in entrances and supporting columns indoors and outdoors throughout New Fantasyland with various appearances. **c.** Acrobats who use chalk for a better grip during their aerial stunts.

21.   **a.** You will see these invention attempts in the queue area and in the garden outside as well as in Maurice's workshop in the cottage.   **b.** You will see Belle's steady growth shown by the marks on the wall. The word "Ans" means years in French.   **c.** A sheep

d. In Maurice's workshop, the gilded mirror seems out of place. This mirror transforms into a magic portal that transports you to the Beast's Castle.   **e.** Everyone is assigned a role during the program.

22.   **a.** There is a carved wooden figurehead of Ariel on the prow of the ship.   **b.** There appear to be three main waterfalls in the area emptying into the tidal pools. There are starfish on the grotto walls and starfish and barnacles on the shipwrecked vessel.   **c.** It is located on the left side of the queue above a tidal pool just before you get to the inside cavern portion of the queue. This was the former location of the popular attraction 20,000 Leagues Under the Sea, which closed in 1994. Disney Imagineers paid tribute to the attraction by carving a silhouette of the *Nautilus* submarine into the rock grotto wall.   **f.** Scuttle is holding a telescope in the queue area. At the beginning of the ride he is playing a type of accordion or squeeze box musical instrument.

23**d.**   A stork

25.   **b.** Star Command, Universe Protection Unit, "beyond."   **c.** Evil Emperor Zurg, robots   **d.** Planet Z

26.   **a.** The large purple display at the entrance reveals that Space Mountain is Starport Seven-Five. **b.** The blue screen monitors near the entrance inform you where the active starports are. There are more active lunar starports than earth starports.   **d.** The threat to the spaceship comes from asteroids.   **f.** The development's name is Constellations-The City of Stars.

Their slogan is "Find Luxury That's out of this Galaxy." Your butler will be a robot.

27a. Experimental Prototype Community of Tomorrow

28. a. It is 18 stories or 180 feet tall and weighs more than 16 million pounds. b. It resembles a golf ball. c. It is considered a geodesic sphere.

30a. Water taken from oceans, lakes, and rivers throughout the world was added to the Fountain of Nations (then known as the Fountain of World Friendship) when the park opened in 1982. Entertaining water ballet shows, with varying musical selections, lighting, and effects take place every 15 minutes.

32. a. International Space Training Center c. X-2 Deep Space Shuttle, Mars e. Landing sites of 30 unmanned and manned missions to the Moon from 1959-76. f. The first men landed on the Moon during the Apollo 11 mission on July 20, 1969.

33. a. Chevrolet c. 65 mph

34. Norway-Maelstrom, Mexico-Gran Fiesta Tour, China-Reflections, France-Impressions

36a. California

37. You ride in the shell of a giant clam.

38. a. The happy starfish is on the wall in the area called "School Friends and Tank Pals." d. Crush calls

our hands "fins" and our shirts "shells." He calls kids "hatchlings" or "little ones." "Dude" is the most popular word in the turtle language.   **e.** A whale

41.   Some notable characters from classic movies found on the crates include Scarlett O'Hara from *Gone with the Wind,* George Bailey from *It's a Wonderful Life*, Rick Blaine from *Casablanca*, Max Bialystock from *The Producers*, and Charles Foster Kane from *Citizen Kane*.

42.   When you pull on the rope at the well you will hear some interesting messages from someone down below. You will hear sounds at the crates as well.

43c.   The scanning droid finds a host of different items when he x-rays the checked luggage. Many of the items are Star Wars or Disney-related, so pay close attention!

44.   **a.** The welcome mat is on the floor below the box office window on the right as you enter.   **b.** The huge dog nose sniffs you and sprays mist on you. **c.** When you pull on the umbrella, water will spray down.   **d.** Some famous stars who left their mark include Harrison Ford, Steve Martin, Audrey Hepburn, Bob Hope, and Jim Henson. Kermit the Frog, R2-D2 and C-3PO, Mickey, Minnie, Goofy, and Donald were also there.   **e.** Props from recent and classic movies are found throughout the queue and change regularly.

45.   **b.** Some classic games represented by board pieces and parts include huge versions of Candy Land, View-Master (Disc), Sorry!, and a Barrel of Monkeys.

There are also giant crayons, dice, dominoes, cards, tinker toys, and Lincoln Logs. **c.** The monkeys come in three colors: yellow, blue and red. They are from the game called Barrel of Monkeys. **d.** The Carnival Barker is Mr. Potato Head voiced by Don Rickles.

47.   **b.** 6, Fender Stratocaster **e.** His black Les Paul guitar **f.** A super stretch limousine

48.   **a.** 199 feet or nearly 20 stories tall. There are multiple drops-the longest is 130 feet or 13 stories. **c.** Lightning hit an elevator on Halloween night 1939 and the five unlucky people inside mysteriously disappeared. **d.** In the hotel lobby there is a cobwebbed owl sculpture surrounded by dead flowers.

50.   **Asia:** Tiger, Komodo Dragon, Eld's Deer, Fruit Bat, Blackbuck Antelope **Africa:** Gorilla, Ball Python, Warthog, Zebra, White Rhinoceros **North America:** Raccoon, Homing Pigeon, Striped Skunk, Corn Snake

53.   *Beauty and the Beast, A Streetcar Named Desire, My Fair Lady, West Side Story*

57.   **a.** Himalayan Escapes, Anandapur Rail Service **e.** Bigfoot or Sasquatch **f.** False-Britton Hill (345 ft.)

58.   **e.** He has gone to Temple. **f.** Rumor has it that he keeps some live geckos as pets.

59d.   The bones you will dig up are mostly from dinosaurs, but sometimes you will find the bones of a Wooly Mammoth. The Wooly Mammoth, an elephant-like mammal, is also extinct but lived long after the dinosaurs.

60.   **a.** Carnotaurus   **b.** The Dino Institute, Iguanodon   **c.** 65 millions years, late Cretaceous Period **d.** A meteor impact, *Deep Impact* and *Armageddon* **f.** There are large American Crocodiles in a walled enclosure near the attraction.

79.   Cast Members can be gloomy at the Haunted Mansion and the Twilight Zone Tower of Terror.

102.   Use an agreed-upon website or GPS device to find the exact distance.

The official GPS address of the Magic Kingdom is: 3111 World Drive., Lake Buena Vista, FL 32830

CLOSING WORD

I designed this book to enhance your Disney vacation with a variety of fun games and activities, but I am not the final word on extra fun at Disney. All visitors to Disney can offer valuable tips from their own personal experiences.

Please send me any suggestions, updates, and ideas for new activities or games, as well as tips or additional comments to my personal email address at slymba@hotmail.com.

I will happily credit you and your family if I use your input in the next version of this book.

Thank you!

Enjoy your Disney vacation!!

INDEX

A

B

C

D

N

O

P

R

S

Y

About the Author

Chris Sylvester has visited Walt Disney World regularly from childhood to adulthood and always transforms into a wide-eyed kid when he is at this magical place. One of his greatest recent achievements was using every means of Disney transportation to visit all four theme parks in one day! His favorite Disney attractions are Space Mountain, Test Track, Twilight Zone Tower of Terror, and Expedition Everest.

Chris is the owner of the tour company DC Capital Kids and the author of *The DC Capital Kids Family Guide to Washington, D.C.*

He lives in the Old Town section of Alexandria, Virginia.